HOME

HOME

EDITED BY MICHAEL J. ROSEN

A Collaboration of Thirty Distinguished Authors
and Illustrators of Children's Books to Aid the Homeless

WRITTEN BY	ILLUSTRATED BY
Franz Brandenberg	Aliki
Mimi Brodsky Chenfield	Karen Barbour
Lucille Clifton	Pat Cummings
Virginia Hamilton	Lisa Desimini
Jamake Highwater	Leo and Diane Dillon
Karla Kuskin	Richard Egielski
Myra Cohn Livingston	Sheila Hamanaka
Liz Rosenberg	James Marshall
Cynthia Rylant	Jerry Pinkney
Jon Scieszka	Vladimir Radunsky
Laurence Yep	James Ransome
Jane Yolen	Aminah Robinson
Arthur Yorinks	Marc Simont
	Lane Smith
	Mary Szilagyi
	Vera B. Williams

A Charlotte Zolotow Book

An Imprint of HarperCollins*Publishers*

illustration by Vera B. Williams

ACKNOWLEDGMENTS

Jacket illustration copyright © 1992 by L. & D. Dillon

Title page illustration copyright © 1992 by Vera B. Williams

Introduction
Copyright © 1992 by Michael J. Rosen
Illustrations copyright © 1992 by Marc Simont

Stoops
Text copyright © 1992 by Mimi Brodsky Chenfield
Illustration copyright © 1992 by
Aminah Brenda L. Robinson

My Bed
Text copyright © 1992 by Franz Brandenberg
Illustrations copyright © 1992 by Aliki Brandenberg

Comfortable Old Chair
Text copyright © 1992 by Karla Kuskin
Illustration copyright © 1992 by Karen Barbour

The Lightwell
Text copyright © 1992 by Laurence Yep
Illustration copyright © 1992 by Sheila Hamanaka

Under the Bed
Text copyright © 1992 by Jon Scieszka
Illustration copyright © 1992 by Lane Smith

Closet
Text copyright © 1992 by Myra Cohn Livingston
Illustration copyright © 1992 by James Ransome

Elevator
Text copyright © 1992 by Lucille Clifton
Illustration copyright © 1992 by Jerry Pinkney

The Refrigerator
Text copyright © 1992 by Arthur Yorinks
Illustration copyright © 1992 by Richard Egielski

The Attic Game
Text copyright © 1992 by Jane Yolen
Illustration copyright © 1992 by James Marshall

Grandmama's Kitchen Table
Text copyright © 1992 by Cynthia Rylant
Illustration copyright © 1992 by Vladimir Radunsky

The Window
Text copyright © 1992 by Liz Rosenberg
Illustration copyright © 1992 by Lisa Desimini

Under the Back Porch
Text copyright © 1992 by Virginia Hamilton
Illustration copyright © 1992 by Pat Cummings

House of Flowers
Text copyright©1992 by The Native Land Foundation
Illustration copyright©1992 by Mary Szilagyi

Home
Copyright © 1992 by HarperCollins Publishers

1 2 3 4 5 6 7 8 9 10
First Edition

Library of Congress Cataloging-in-Publication Data
Home / edited by Michael J. Rosen.
    p.   cm.
    "A Charlotte Zolotow book."
    Summary: Thirteen authors and seventeen illustrators celebrate the places and
things that make up the home, in support of Share Our Strength's (SOS) fight against
homelessness.
    ISBN 0-06-021788-X. — ISBN 0-06-021789-8 (lib. bdg.)
    I. Homelessness—Literary collections.   2. Children's literature.
[I. Homelessness—Literary collections.   Literature—Collections.]
I. Rosen, Michael J., date.
PZ5.H748   1992
810.8' 0355—dc20   91-29125
                                                                    CIP
                                                                    AC

Home is what you take away each time you leave the house. Like a wristwatch, it ticks beside the ticking that is your heart. Whether or not you hear it, look at its face, or feel its hold, *We're with you* is what the minute, hour, and second hands of home have to tell.

Home is the place that goes where you go, yet it welcomes you upon your return. Like a dog overjoyed at the door, *We've missed you* is what you hear, no matter how long you've been gone.

Home is all the things you know by name: a family of dishes, books, and clothes that waits for you to choose among them every day. *We're ready for you* is what the chorus in your house sings. Your fingerprints are grinning on their faces.

And home is all the names that know you, the one and only person who does just what you do. Home is all the words that call you in for dinner, over to help, into a hug, out of a dream.

Come in, come in, wherever you've been. . . .
This is the poem in which you're a part.
This is the home that knows you by heart.

—Michael J. Rosen
illustration by Marc Simont

STOOPS
by Mimi Brodsky Chenfield
illustrated by Aminah Robinson

My name is Anna and this is my seat on the third step of our stoop. Next stoop, Sammy and Pedro play stoop ball. The other kids jump double Dutch and play hopscotch and bouncy balls on the street. I am waiting for Kim.

"Hurry, Kim! I got something to tell you," I holler up.

"What?" she hollers down from her fourth-floor window.

"I'll tell you when you come down," I yell. "Bring your jacks—I forgot mine."

Pedro and Sam throw the ball, it misses the step, it bounces into Mrs. Shapiro's lap, and she says, "Careful, boys."

She tosses it back and goes on talking to Mrs. Gomez.

I scoot over to let Mrs. Brown by, as she bumps her grocery bags past me.

"Come on, Kim," I call again up to her window.

The jump-rope kids jump.

"Come on, Kim," they yell.

Kim's aunt puts her head out the window.

"Not till she cleans the table," she calls.

"Clean it, Kim," I yell.

"Clean it, Kim," Pedro and Sammy tease.

"Clean it," the hopscotch kids call, hopping from square to square.

"Clean it." The jump-rope kids jump with each swing of the rope.

"Clean it," the bouncing ball kids chant with each bounce of the ball.

"Tell your secret, Anna." The kids begin to clap,
and now it is a song, a song about jump rope and jacks,
hopscotch and bouncing balls,
   and the secrets of friends
      playing on the stoop
         of home.

♥ MY BED ♥
by Franz Brandenberg
illustrated by Aliki

I am the king in my castle.

I am a mole in a hole.

I am a train in a tunnel.

I am a pirate in a den.

I am an explorer in a cave.

I am a lion tamer in a circus tent.

I am a bear asleep in my lair.

Good night.

COMFORTABLE OLD CHAIR
by Karla Kuskin
illustrated by Karen Barbour

A bird has a nest
A fox has a lair
A den is home
If you're a bear.
I have a comfortable old chair.

Soft pillowed blue,
a flowered cloud.
The perfect place to read aloud
to myself or silently
letting long words run over me,
letting the stories I have read
make moving pictures in my head.
New chairs are nice
but mine is best.
My spot to think in
brood in
rest
to plot in
dream in, many dreams,
to scheme a few outlandish schemes in.
Kings need crowns to be the king
but me
I can be anything
any person
anywhere
if I just have my book and chair.

THE LIGHTWELL
by Laurence Yep
illustrated by Sheila Hamanaka

My grandmother lives in a tiny studio apartment in Chinatown. Her home, in the rear of the building, receives no direct sunlight even though her window opens on a lightwell; for the lightwell seems to stretch endlessly upward and downward among the many buildings. At its brightest, it is filled with a kind of tired twilight.

Although the lightwell is a poor source for light, it is a perfect carrier for sound. In the mornings it carries sound from all the other apartments—the slap of wet laundry being hung in a window, the rush of water into a sink, the crying of a baby. During the afternoons, bits of conversation float into my grandmother's home like fragments of little dramas and comedies—just as, I'm sure, the other tenants can hear the shuffling of my grandmother's cards and her exclamations when she loses at solitaire.

Toward evening, as my grandmother clanks pots on her stove, I can hear matching sounds from the other apartments as her neighbors also prepare their meals. And the smell of my grandmother's simmering rice and frying vegetables mingles with the other smells in the lightwell until there are enough aromas for a banquet.

Side by side, top and below, each of us lives in our own separate time and space. And yet we all belong to the same building, our lives touching however briefly and faintly.

UNDER THE BED
by Jon Scieszka
illustrated by Lane Smith

There are all these things under my bed.

I know. I'm supposed to clean them out today.

But what do you do with three checkers, one sock, a marble, and a dragon?

Where do you put a green necklace, pirate treasure, magic rings?

Then there's my submarine, spaceship, jet, and time machine.

My cave, my castle, my treehouse, my fort. Wild horses, genies, monsters, magicians. Two-headed serpents, black knights, vikings, and cowboys.

And what's a guy to do with his jungle, his ocean, the top of Mount Everest? Five dust balls, half a cookie, and one unexplored galaxy?

Where do all of these things go? I don't know.

But there are all these things under my bed.

I know.

CLOSET
by Myra Cohn Livingston
illustrated by James Ransome

Under the stairs, a secret cave
heaped with treasure waits for me,
waits for my *Open, Sesame!*

I turn the knob. The brown door creaks.
I shine my flashlight. Looming shapes—
forty thieves wrapped in dusty capes
hail my return. I crouch and count
ingots of silver, bars of gold,
all that my robber fingers hold.

Brocades and silks from strange bazaars,
translucent pearls and diamonds bright
glitter with my beam of light.
I reach for the doorknob, making sure
I can escape if anyone dares
tread on my cave roof, under the stairs.

ELEVATOR
by Lucille Clifton
illustrated by Jerry Pinkney

down
in the corner
my book and i
traveling
over the project
walls
so the world
is more than this
elevator
stuck between
floors again
and home
is a corner
where i crouch
safe
reading waiting
to start moving
up

THE REFRIGERATOR
by Arthur Yorinks
illustrated by Richard Egielski

Hey, it's where it's all happening. It's a hum. It's a vibration. It's cool, it's crazy. It's the box, the chiller, the freeze machine, the Frigidaire. Wow.

Listen now. Open the door and it's a symphony. A jazz treat. Look, the eggs are keeping the beat. The milk's shakin', so is the bacon. It's a food apartment house: rocking and rolling, slinking and snaking. The carrots are stomping, the cabbage is romping, even the cheese is having a good time.

Catch those hot dogs belting a tune? Wait 'til you hear, the leftover chicken can really croon. The jellies are jamming, the ham is hamming—that's right, the sour pickles are twisting and shouting with joy.

At the top it's the peak, the penthouse, the ultimate ice, yes, that's right, it's the freezer. There's frozen fries, apple pies, yesterday's pizza, the ole geezer. Cubes are swinging, pops are swaying, the peas are popping, the string beans are bopping. . . . It's frost free, I'm told, where nobody minds the cold.

Upstairs, downstairs, in a drawer, on a shelf, small compartment, large compartment, what a place to live the refrigerator is, that is, if you're a cucumber.

THE ATTIC GAME
by Jane Yolen
illustrated by James Marshall

My brother thinks the attic
Is a very spooky place,
With webs as thick as dental floss
That bang against his face.

My sister thinks the attic
Is a place where darkness grows
Until it makes big shadow patches
Over all her clothes.

But me—I think the attic
Is the place I love the most,
Where I can be a wizard,
An explorer, or a ghost,

A doctor saving patients,
Or an astronaut in space,
A pirate on the briny deep,
A cop hot on a case.

For everything I'll ever need
To play my attic selves
Is stuffed in boxes, bags, and trunks
Upon our attic shelves.

GRANDMAMA'S KITCHEN TABLE
by Cynthia Rylant
illustrated by Vladimir Radunsky

Since I was four years old I have been talking about my life to the people who sit at my grandmama's kitchen table in Cool Ridge, West Virginia.

The kitchen is small and skinny. There is a little window next to Grandmama's table, and this is where she sits when she is alone in the house. Out it she can see the birds at the apple tree, eating the seed she left them, and she can see who's driving up the hollow, or whose child is walking out the dirt road to the school bus. There are woods all around, and her eyes will follow them down past the creek, down past Bill Mills' house, and on.

When I am visiting, I make sure I never sit in Grandmama's chair. I want her to have her little window.

Relatives will come by—Uncle Dean and Aunt Linda, Sue and the girls, Bev and the baby—and all sit around Grandmama's sturdy old table, even though someone will have to sit on a bench in the doorway or on an extra chair that will block anybody who's trying to get through the room. But no one wants to go into the living room, where there's plenty seats for us all. We want to be in Grandmama's kitchen, near this heavy old table, and we want to drink coffee and tea and Coke and eat angel food cake or leftover biscuits and talk and talk and talk and talk until we are all talked out, and there is nothing left to do but go on home and rest up and come back tomorrow to talk some more.

THE WINDOW
by Liz Rosenberg
illustrated by Lisa Desimini

I hear the cows lowing
across the fields.
They sound like an ocean
standing still.
I can stand still and follow
the path the wind makes
as it slides through the grass.
And there is the hollow
where I once saw a deer
standing up to his ankles in the snow —
then flash past the barn
through a hole in the trees
like a piece of white wool
passing into a needle. If I stare
at the glass, I can see a pale face
with dark shining eyes
looking out at the world
from her bedroom window.

UNDER THE BACK PORCH
by Virginia Hamilton
illustrated by Pat Cummings

Our house is two stories high
shaped like a white box.
There is a yard stretched around it
and in back
a wooden porch.

Under the back porch is my place.
I rest there.
I go there when I have to be alone.
It is always shaded and damp.
Sunlight only slants through the slats
in long strips of light,
and the smell of the damp
is moist green,
like the moss that grows here.

My sisters and brothers
can stand on the back porch
and never know
I am here
underneath.
It is my place.
All mine.

HOUSE OF FLOWERS
by Jamake Highwater
illustrated by Mary Szilagyi

In a sunny bed of fragrant earth
  the garden makes love.
Twisting slowly against a luminous breeze
  she spreads her hair
  like sprinklers on the summer lawn.
When time makes its long song
  the garden's many-colored children are born
beneath a fragile shelter of leaves.
Cauliflowers and butterflies,
  roses, sparrows, and weeds.
Precious dwellers of the grass,
  creatures great and small.
In the evening, with the drumming of the moon,
  they cling to one another,
Dreaming of a house made of flowers
  and warm in the garden's safe embrace.

illustration by Marc Simont

Come in, come in, wherever you've been . . . .
This is the poem in which you're a part.
This is the poem that knows you by heart.